GRAVITY HILLS

This series features unsolved mysteries, urban legends, and other curious stories. Each creepy, shocking, or befuddling book focuses on what people believe and hear. True or not? That's for you to decide!

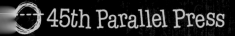
45th Parallel Press

Published in the United States of America by Cherry Lake Publishing
Ann Arbor, Michigan
www.cherrylakepublishing.com

Author: Virginia Loh-Hagan
Reading Adviser: Marla Conn MS, Ed., Literacy specialist, Read-Ability, Inc.
Book Designer: Felicia Macheske

Photo Credits: © Maksim Toome/Shutterstock.com, cover; © Shannon Shepard/Shutterstock.com, 5; © Redakie/
Shutterstock.com, 7; © Peter Titmuss/Shutterstock.com, 8; © MBR9292/Shutterstock.com, 11;© kenny1/
Shutterstock.com, 13; © Everett Historical/Shutterstock.com, 15; © mike.irwin/Shutterstock.com, 16; © Annette
Shaff/Shutterstock.com, 19; © Pefkos/Shutterstock.com, 20; © ktsimage/istock, 23; © Susan Schmitz/
Shutterstock.com, 25; © Iryna VK/Shutterstock.com, 26; © InnervisionArt/Shutterstock.com, 29

Graphic Elements Throughout: © iofoto/Shutterstock.com; © COLCU/Shutterstock.com; © spacedrone808/
Shutterstock.com; © rf.vector.stock/Shutterstock.com; © donatas1205/Shutterstock.com; © cluckva/
Shutterstock.com; © Eky Studio/Shutterstock.com

45th Parallel Press is an imprint of Cherry Lake Publishing.

Library of Congress Cataloging-in-Publication Data

Names: Loh-Hagan, Virginia, author.
Title: Gravity Hills / by Dr. Virginia Loh-Hagan.
Description: Ann Arbor : Cherry Lake Publishing, 2018. | Series: Urban
legends: don't read alone! | Audience: Grade 4 to 6. | Includes
bibliographical references and index.
Identifiers: LCCN 2017033728| ISBN 9781534107625 (hardcover) | ISBN
9781534109605 (pdf) | ISBN 9781534108615 (pbk.) | ISBN 9781534120594
(hosted ebook)
Subjects: LCSH: Optical illusions—Juvenile literature. | Geographical
myths—Juvenile literature.
Classification: LCC QP495 .L64 2018 | DDC 152.14/8—dc23
LC record available at https://lccn.loc.gov/2017033728

Cherry Lake Publishing would like to acknowledge the work of The Partnership for 21st Century Skills.
Please visit *www.p21.org* for more information.

Printed in the United States of America
Corporate Graphics

TABLE OF CONTENTS

Chapter One

BLAMING GHOSTS!

What happened at Antioch? What happened at Livermore? What happened at Kyamwilu?

Antioch **Gravity** Hill is near San Francisco, California. Gravity is a special force. It pulls things down. A woman and her friends went to the hill. They did this in 2003. The woman said, "I was scared out of my mind! Our car was moved at least 25 feet uphill." This happens a lot.

Some people think ghosts move their cars. It's believed that children died at this hill. The children's ghosts push cars uphill. They don't want others to get hurt. These children were in a school bus. There were heavy rains. Their bus slid. Everyone drowned.

There's an empty slaughterhouse and a hospital for insane people near Antioch. This makes the story scarier.

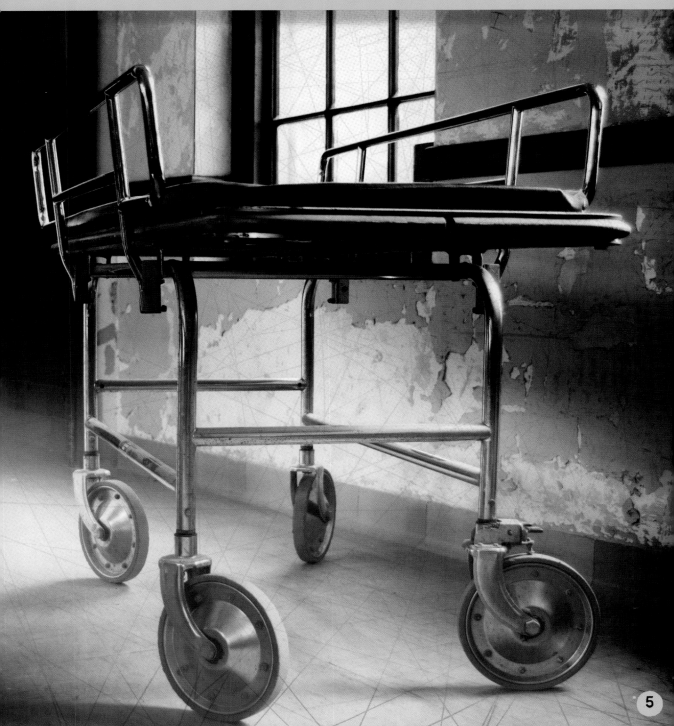

CONSIDER THE EVIDENCE

There's a gravity hill in North Carolina. It's on Stewartsville Cemetery Road. Something strange happens there. Cars at the bottom of the hill will gently roll backward. They'll roll up the hill. Lumbees live in this area. They're a Native American group that mixed with other groups. Some think they're linked to the lost Roanoke colonists. They believe in ghosts. They believe a mother, her daughter, and their dog were killed there. Their car stopped. A truck hit them. They believe the mother's ghost is pushing cars uphill. Cliff Sessoms is the assistant chief of the police department. He said, "I have gone and put my car in neutral and seen it roll back up the hill."

Livermore Gravity Hill is in California. People hear sounds. They hear footsteps. They see handprints on their cars. They feel their cars being pushed uphill.

Two high school students' ghosts push the cars. The students came home from a dance. They drove off the road. They died. Some believe their ghosts push cars away. They don't want to be bothered.

Other people believe football players' ghosts push the cars. Two football players were out at night. They got their clothes stolen. They died from the cold. They **haunt** the area. Haunt means to bother.

Strange things happen to cars at Livermore Gravity Hill.

Three people are buried at Kyamwilu Hills.

Kyamwilu Hills is in Kenya, Africa. Cars roll uphill. They speed up on their own. People lose their breath walking downhill. Water flows uphill.

People believe the place is haunted. There were two brothers. Their names were Kyalo and Mwilu. They both married the same girl from another area. Kyalo lived at the bottom of the hill. Mwilu lived at the top. The men became jealous. They fought over the woman. They all died. The brothers were buried where they lived. The woman was buried halfway up the hill. Some people think their strange relationship caused the hill's strange forces. People say they see their ghosts. The ghosts are dressed in white robes.

Chapter Two

FORCEFUL HILLS

What are gravity hills? Where are they located?

Gravity hills are strange slopes. Things seem to move against gravity. They do this on their own. On gravity hills, things roll uphill. This is odd. Things are supposed to roll downhill. Gravity hills are places where the laws of gravity don't seem to apply.

Gravity hills are also called **magnetic** hills. Magnetic means having a strong force that attracts. Gravity hills are also called **mystery** hills. Certain areas are called mystery spots. Mystery means unknown.

Magnetic forces are at play at gravity hills.

SPOTLIGHT

BIOGRAPHY

Rachel Miller is a tour guide supervisor. She works at the Santa Cruz Mystery Spot. This mystery spot is in the Redwood Forest in California. It's a 150-foot (46 meter) circle. Strange things happen in this circle. People can't stand straight there. They have to lean. Miller said, "The hill was extremely difficult to walk up." There seems to be a force pushing back on people's chests. Miller likes telling visitors about the spot. She likes seeing how confused they are. She likes hearing them figure things out. She said, "We've had scientists come out, and they haven't found anything strange with the plants, animals, soil, or air. There's nothing off-balance." She gives 45-minute tours. She's very busy. She feels the force every day.

Gravity hills are in many parts of the world. Many are in the United States. There are hundreds of gravity hills.

Gravity hills are located on **paved** roads. Paved means they've been covered. The roads are short. They're usually a few hundred feet long. The road looks like it's going uphill.

Gravity hills are located in areas with strange land features. They also seem to be near death. Some are by **cemeteries**. Cemeteries are where people are buried. People may have crashed there. People may have died there.

Sometimes the roads near gravity hills are called "magic roads."

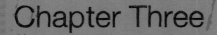

Chapter Three

IT'S SHOWTIME!

When did gravity hills become popular?
How do gravity hills provide entertainment?

The Great **Depression** took place in the 1930s.
The Depression was a sad period in history. Many
people lost their jobs. People lost a lot of money. Many
people became poor. They were out of work. They were
hungry. They were homeless. Many people moved west.
They moved to California.

People needed some fun. They needed to escape their sad lives. They wanted **entertainment**. Entertainment is shows. Shows amuse people. They make people happy.

During the 1930s, many moved west looking for work.

Crooked houses were built near gravity hills.

Gravity hills became popular during this time. They were easy. The hills were already there. Some people built special houses in this area. The houses were built on slants. They created tricks. They let people walk on walls. They showed chairs hanging on walls. They showed water flowing uphill. They showed cars rolling uphill.

People charged a fee. Visitors came. They saw. They wondered about gravity. They were amazed. They forgot their troubles for a bit.

People still visit these spots today. But they visit to be scared. They visit to see ghosts.

REAL-WORLD
CONNECTION

Trampolines are sheets attached to springs. People jump up and down on them. There's a new extreme sport. It's called "wall trampoline." People who do it call themselves bouncers. Bouncers hurl themselves off a wall. They land on a trampoline. They snap back toward the wall. They flip. They twist. They can jump over 16 feet (5 m). Wall trampoline is part gymnastics. It's part parkour. Parkour is an extreme sport. It's when people climb walls. They do flips. Wall trampoline is also popular at circus school. Bouncers want wall trampoline to be in the X Games. People who do extreme sports try to defy gravity. They push limits.

Chapter Four

BEYOND GHOSTS

What are some explanations for the strange things that happen at gravity hills?

People have many **explanations**. Explanations are ideas. They have different ways to explain gravity hills. People want to figure out why strange things happen at these hills.

Ghost children are the most popular explanation for gravity hills. This is the most common story: Children are in a school bus. The bus stops working. The children help push the bus uphill. The bus rolls backward. It rolls over the children. The children die. Their ghosts haunt gravity hills.

People have reported fingerprints on their cars.

Earth may be to blame. Some people think big magnets are buried under the hills. These magnets pull things up. Some people believe there's a **vortex**. A vortex is spinning air. It sucks things in. Part of this vortex is above ground. Part of it is below ground.

Some people blame aliens. They think aliens have buried their tools under the hills. The tools are metal cones. They're alien magnets. Some people believe aliens are directing their spaceships to land on gravity hills.

The alien tools help them navigate.

INVESTIGATION TIPS

- Talk to someone who has been to a gravity hill. Ask them questions. Find out what it was like.

- Bring baby powder. Sprinkle it on your car. Look for handprints left by ghosts.

- Get mapping equipment. Measure the difference between the top and bottom of the hill.

- Bring a level. This is a builder's tool. It lets you know if lines and edges are straight. It makes sure lines and edges are horizontal. Horizontal means going in the same direction of the ground.

- Bend over. Look at the slope through your legs. This changes your reference point. It lets you see how things really are.

Some people think aliens buried their spaceships under gravity hills. The spaceships are giving off dangerous rays. These rays are messing with gravity.

Some people think a **meteor** fell. Meteors are space rocks. They hit the earth. They broke into pieces. They glow. Meteor bits fell on gravity hills. They made a "magic circle."

Some people think gravity hills are time **warps**. A warp is a curve in something straight. They think the hills mess with space and time. This means people move from one time period to another.

Alien spaceships are called UFOs, or unidentified flying objects.

Chapter Five

SCIENCE VS. STORY

What is a story that tells how gravity hills formed? What is the scientific explanation for gravity hills?

There are different explanations for what causes gravity hills. There are also different explanations for how gravity hills were formed.

There's a gravity hill in Lake Wales, Florida. It's called Spook Hill. Many years ago, a giant alligator raided the town. It was 17 feet (5 m) long. It ate people. It attacked every night. People were scared. A Native American chief prayed to the Forces of Nature. He fought the alligator. The Forces helped him kill the alligator. But the Forces never left. They stayed to mess with gravity.

A monster alligator terrorized a town in Florida.

The placement of plants and trees could also trick the eyes.

People love telling stories. It's hard for science to compete with an alligator war.

Scientists say that gravity hills are **optical illusions**. Optical refers to things we see. Illusions are fake images. Gravity hills are tricks of the eyes. People see what they want to see.

Gravity hills are special places. The land makes a downhill slope look uphill. The **layout** makes this image. Layout means how the land is designed.

EXPLAINED BY SCIENCE

Gravity is a force. It tries to pull two objects toward each other. Anything that has mass has a gravitational pull. Gravity gives things weight. It pulls on all the mass in an object. Gravity is important. All objects have gravity. Some objects have more gravity than others. Earth has gravity. Its gravity keeps us on the ground. It keeps us from flying away. It causes objects to fall. It holds the moon in orbit around the Earth. The sun has gravity. Its gravity holds the planets in orbit around the sun. Life on Earth needs the sun's light and warmth. Gravity keeps Earth at the right distance from the sun. Too close and it'd be too hot. Too far and it'd be too cold.

Gravity hills have **angular** things around them. Angular means having lots of lines. It means not curvy. There could be rocks with straight edges. There could be rows of trees that make lines.

Gravity hills hide the **horizon**. Horizon is the line where the earth and sky meet. People have a weird perspective. They can't compare things to the horizon. They can't see what's level. They can't judge the slope.

All these things work together. They make eyes see **inclines** instead of **declines**. Inclines are lines that go up. Declines are lines that go down.

Real or not? It doesn't matter. Gravity hills live in people's imaginations.

People's eyes and brains don't read visual signs correctly.

DID YOU KNOW?

There's a gravity hill in Pennsylvania. It has a long name. It's known as "Just off Route 219 in Brandy Camp, Elk County." People think it's haunted. They think horse ghosts live there.

Mars is smaller than Earth. It has less mass than Earth. It has less gravity. One hundred pounds (45 kilograms) on Earth is 38 pounds (17 kg) on Mars.

There are researchers at the University of Padova and the University of Pavia. They studied gravity hills. They did this in 2003. They made a fake gravity hill. They used boards. They put boards at different angles. They had people look at the boards. They found it's easy to make people see something as uphill. They found it's hard to make people see it as downhill. They found that not having a horizon affects how we see things.

Priest Hill is in Southern California. Some people believe in a ghost story. A priest's car broke down. The priest stepped out. He prayed. A car hit him. The priest died. His ghost helps others by pushing their cars.

Whittier Gravity Hill is near Los Angeles, California. It's in a cemetery. The hill is in rose gardens. People's cars roll uphill. People hear strange knocking noises. Cars at the top don't roll downhill. People have reported seeing alien spaceships and devil worshippers.

Another popular story involves escaped prisoners. These prisoners kill children in a school bus. The children's ghosts haunt gravity hills.

The opposite of gravity hills is "false flats." This is when something uphill looks flat. Bikers see these a lot.

CONSIDER THIS!

Take a Position: Some people turn gravity hills into tours. They turn them into a business. They charge people to visit. Do you think people should make money off gravity hills? Argue your point with reasons and evidence.

Say What? Summarize what you learned from this book. Then find a gravity hill near you. Visit it. Describe your experience. Compare it to your own experience.

Think About It! Why do people question science? Why would some people prefer to believe in aliens rather than science?

LEARN MORE

- Claybourne, Anna. *Gut-Wrenching Gravity and Other Fatal Forces*. New York: Crabtree Publishing Company, 2013.

- Omoth, Tyler. *Handbook to Stonehenge, the Bermuda Triangle, and Other Mysterious Locations*. North Mankato, MN: Capstone Press, 2017.

- Rooney, Anne. *You Wouldn't Want to Live Without Gravity!* New York: Franklin Watts, 2016.

GLOSSARY

angular (ANG-gyuh-lur) not curvy, having lots of lines

cemeteries (SEM-ih-ter-eez) places where dead bodies are buried

declines (DEE-klinez) lines that go down, downhill

Depression (dih-PRESH-uhn) a time when many people lost their jobs

entertainment (en-tur-TAYN-muhnt) shows that amuse people

explanations (ek-spluh-NAY-shuhnz) ideas that explain something

gravity (GRAV-ih-tee) force that pulls two objects toward each other

haunt (HAWNT) to bother, to hang out

horizon (huh-RYE-zuhn) the line where the sky and the earth meet

illusions (ih-LOO-zhuhnz) fake images

inclines (IN-klinez) lines that go up, uphill

layout (LAY-out) how something is designed

magnetic (mag-NET-ik) having a strong force that attracts

meteor (MEE-tee-or) space rock that hits the earth and then breaks into pieces that glow

mystery (MIS-tur-ee) unknown

optical (AHP-tih-kuhl) of the eyes, vision

paved (PAYVD) covered with concrete, tar, or asphalt

vortex (VOR-teks) spinning air that sucks things in

warps (WORPS) curves that develop in something straight

INDEX

ABOUT THE AUTHOR

Dr. Virginia Loh-Hagan is an author, university professor, former classroom teacher, and curriculum designer. From writing this book, she learned there are several gravity hills near her home. She lives in San Diego with her very tall husband and very naughty dogs. To learn more about her, visit www.virginialoh.com.